M000299909

The Cutting Songs
of the Butcher Son

Poems by Michael Cissell

Kansas City   Spartan Press   Missouri

Spartan Press
Kansas City, Missouri
spartanpresskc.com

Spartan
Press

Design, edits and layout: Jason Ryberg
Cover image: Rob Compton
Author photo: Darrah Walker

Spartan Press would like to thank Prospero's Books,
The Fellowship of N-finite Jest, The Prospero Institute
of Disquieted P/o/e/t/i/c/s, Will Leathem, Tom Wayne,
Jeanette Powers, j. d. tulloch, Jon Bidwell, Jason Preu,
Mark McClane, Tony Hayden and the whole Osage Arts
Community.

The Butcher Son would like to blame the following people
for bringing this book into existence: The Butcher and the
Butcher Lady, Stephen Johnson, Albert Goldbarth,
Jason Ryberg. Thanks.

A few of the poems here have been previously featured
in the following publications:

"How to Scream a Fish," "After Weariness," "Wallace Stevens
Elizabeth Bishop My Friends and I at Land Between
the Lakes" first appeared in *Open 24 Hrs;* "Meat for Natural
Hunger" and "Graceland" first appeared in *Mikrocosmos*
and later in *Open 24 Hrs.* and "Butcher Son Cuts on Language"
appeared in *The Sheridan Review* under a different title.

CONTENTS

This book is dedicated
to my wife Monica and
my sons Guthrie and
Rohan — my life blood

Overture

The Butcher Son a child already the fool
forgot his name told his name sometimes
Terri sometimes Chris sometimes Steve
and all them fools Butcher Son believe and call
him many whom him are not and Butcher Son say
Yes. To them all. And to them all he play.

Even today them fools do ask,
What the face behind the mask?
Who now, Old Nick? Who now, Old Bone?
Be him the bloated drunk and purse-snatch
balloon-belly Jack who a pint and a ho
sell his soul then cheat the Devil his own?

Be him the yellow stocking dancing man
who friends did play as on a lute and
cry in dark alone love create me fool?
Be him language monster Caliban
whose pregnant tongue his lord did ban
from seeding the world in demons cruel?

Who now, Sometimes Nick? Who now, Tambo?
Be him blackface minstrel grandfather who
argue notes down stage from Brother Bones?
The prattling poet who on the plains of Kansas
his UFO in burning wheat fields crashed
to show the hoi polloi their weedy souls?

Who now, Foolish Boy? Who now, Shadow?
The Jewish grandfather? His dying Prince? God Himself?
All. Butcher Son say. Again. All. Though
on vibrations of your private thoughts be felt
my cutting songs and hate me and throw
me bones The Butcher Son all. To show.

I

The Butcher

*The butcher-boy puts off his killing-clothes, or sharpens
his knife at the stall in the market, I loiter,
enjoying his repartee and his shuffle and break-down.*

—Walt Whitman, *Song of Myself*

*Then he brought forward the second ram, the ordination
ram, and Aaron and his sons laid their hands on its head.
When he had slaughtered it, Moses took some of its blood
and put it on the tip of Aaron's right ear, on the thumb of his
right hand, and on the big toe of his right foot.*

—Leviticus 8:22

Voices

I.

The dark bones of the underground grandfather
lie black beneath the bluegrass.
Butcher Son found them once.
Deep inside his own muscle.
And the bones spoke. Their voice is blood.

II.

Butcher Son grandmother heard angels.
They whispered their hosannas,
murmured their hallelujahs,
hummed their litanies into the DNA fiber gut-wall
of her womanhood. They wove her chromosones
into rosaries. They sowed her sacred heart
to circulate the immaculate blood
through the unsullied veins of her unborn *mishpocha*.
And the grandmother whispered back. Supplicated
before the seraphic host, closed her curtains, closed
her doors to the push and pulse of the world,
cloistered inside her Catholic grubstake.

III.

When Butcher Son fell from the willow,
the branches, like devils' whips,
lashed his legs and face and back
until he hit the earth hard.
Like a terrified angel.
Some blood, some bruises.
His breath left him.
And the universe fell away.
His bones,
like the naked coffee tree,
solid and strong.

IV.

And the universe fell away,
Butcher Son grandmother said.
And there he sat. Lucifer himself. Smack dab
on the foot of my bed. Butcher Son believed
because Mee-maw spoke to the fathers
of St. Francis Catholic Church who housed her
in a low-rent government piece.
They saw her there. And for her repentance,
and her admittance the grandmother dusted
the pews, polished the altar,
cleaned the rectory and restrooms,

wiped away the dirt inside the wounds
on Christ's plastic body. She knew secrets.
She heard angels. *On the foot of my bed.*
She rocked, swayed in jubilation.
Satan laid on that night, boy.
His black scent smelled like creek bottom.
They say the devil's blood red, but I tell you
he's the color of the falling sun,
A fading brightness. A darkness inside light.
But I wasn't afraid, child. Not your Mee-maw.
Because I felt the Lord's angelic host behind me.
And that Devil he's pathetic. Sorrowful.
Bigger than we meant Him to be.
'Get thee gone, Devil, I sang, and he slid away.
The old snake. I tell you, boy,
Your grandmother's heel was hard
on Satan that day your grandfather died.
When your dad was eight,
like you."

V.

And dead I am Butcher Son. Dead as da flesh
dat killed me. Dead and buried in da bluegrass
under da hills where I rustle and whisper behind
you and chill da bones dat built you. Butcher Son
yer gonna tussle. Yer gonna squabble.

Yer gonna struggle. Lust and hate and love.

Yer hard music and yer harder tongue no pardon.

But I find yer constitution suitable.

Da Devil is bigger dan we meant and he ain't gone.

Buck up, Butcher Son. Transmutable.

Da universe falling away. Da universe on da run.

Flesh and Blood

Beef brings out the best in us.

—Frank Menches

I.

Having plastered Paducah's walls
and caulked the city's cracks,
sealed whatever leakage that seeped

through walls and churches,
Butcher Son grandfather, 1956,
arrived home to meat-heavy table

Butcher Son grandmother set
only an hour before
—she home from 8-hour knee-bent day

scrubbing the church rectory
to seal the Cissell fiscal tear—
corked his coronary walls with roast wax

and pork and died before the dinner table.
Butcher Son uncle, 1958, drowned in Ohio
and a month later, a Kroger semi

housing the frozen flesh of every animal
fortunate to book passage aboard the Ark,
spread Butcher Son aunt across pavement

like A-1; and Butcher Son father The Butcher,
begins his butcher-boy apprenticeship at Bigg's
in the aesthetics of cutting and shaping .

II.

And that's all Butcher Son really know except
at eighteen The Butcher met The Butcher Lady
and one *a do ron ron ron* rockabilly night

in Wimpy Grill they sashayed boothward, linked
like Braunschweiger sausage, delicately decorated
as dinner tables (her plump buns *a la cha-cha* gamboled

so sweetly beneath her poodle skirt The Butcher's
loins boiled) and discovered over a few juicy nibbles
of Wimpy Grill double bacon cheeseburgers

their glyphs, their alchemy, their recipes.
They're as cozy together as bun and beef.
He promised The Butcher Lady the most tender

cuts of rolled flank, short loin (boned and boneless)
hind shank and brisket. For her a heart-stamped menu
and the rarest rolled rump porterhouse bottom round.

He'd top chuck roll, bottom chuck roll, shoulder arm
neck roll, grill, broil, bake, fry any busting red meat
her red lips quivered for. Yes. He'd give it to her.

III.

Butcher Son see years in albums
buried in The Butcher's bedroom
like Egyptian hieroglyphs entombed

1970 wedding reception banquet table
laden as greasy and heavy as The Butcher's
father's death table with beef scaloppini

stuffed with chicken, pork-stuffed green peppers,
potato salad diced salami and burgers. Oh! Burgers!
Oh! This their love-meat! This their love-pucker!

The Farmer's Burger under mushroom gravy.
Red-eye bacon and egg jalapeno burger.
A-1 Burger, Kentucky Bourbon Burger baked.

Such flesh! Such eternal beefy promises!
Such perturbations as later The Butcher cut
Kroger's carcasses—his life wrapped in paper
his apron blood-stained and stiff like corpses
The Butcher baptized in flesh and blood
at the butcher block altar.

And The Butcher Son unwombed
a bloody fool who believe him not The Butcher
who sometime believe him not flesh and blood.

The Butcher's Love Song

I love the slap of short loin on my block,
the tingle in my teeth when my carving knife

splits the cut and separates the porterhouse,
and the red smell of tenderloin and T-bone, two

flesh-woven meats: they are grace; they are divinity;
they compose the prayer of my day.

The Butcher's Hands

My hands in the bowels
of a gutted cow
are God's hands in the world.
What I feel, God feels.

After Weariness

Nine hours today The Butcher cut for Kroger
its porterhouse and T-bone steaks.
At home The Butcher stands before his block;

a deer hangs from girders. The Butcher
has stripped its skin, sawed away its head
and legs and this is The Butcher's world,

the world of grownups he wears in blood
carries on his breath. The world Butcher Son refuse
to enter, who's home from school to his world

of *Greek Stories and Roman Tales for Children*
Gods of Norsemen and *Dragon Stories*
and Thor, the god of thunder and labor,

Mirmir held high in work and paean
against the giants. Jason's golden fleece.
The Minotaur's insatiable need for flesh.

Butcher Son carries heroes and monsters
to The Butcher's world, where The Butcher
measures and shears for The Butcher's world,

where Butcher Son stands with shield his father
cut from cardboard and bow and arrow he carved
from sticks the great Odysseus would proudly brandish

The Butcher's world, where he asks Butcher Son
to write cut names on packages and Butcher Son
refuse and The Butcher lifts his face

to his face and Butcher Son smells the blood,
the flesh. He smell fatigue. He read
a dragon. Picture from story books.

Meat for Natural Hunger

What we have here is The Butcher Son who reads
Niitzsche, discusses *The Inferno* and *Paradise Lost*
as the The Butcher rolls the carcass quarter-ward.

An existentialist who deconstructs Christians
as The Butcher separates the hindquarter's primal
cuts, plunges his knife into flesh that can't bleed,

speaks of serving cheap round steak to Vietnam
recruits who were later cut to pieces and bombed.
Butcher Son say the bourgeoisie are real butchers.

The Butcher removes the short loin from hindquarter
and curses his shrapnel scar the gray of steel,
carves with definitude the Delmonico and T-bone

and porterhouse. The Butcher Son sees the steaks
of Rodin's nude *Danaid*. Her marble flesh filet.
The Butcher speaks to the death of the butcher,

killed by pre-packing plants in Chicago and Kansas City,
meat tinctured the diseased yellow of jaundice
and the debasement of the industry under Reagan.

The Butcher likes best to break it all down, display,
a free-standing statue, and maybe it's absurd
vanity of work—the making of a thing—

but The Butcher studies his cuts and wipes his blade
clean and his language Butcher Son reads
is clean cut, tender, and all too human.

The Butcher Son Blues

My daddy was a butcher, my mama praise the Lord.
My daddy was a butcher, my mama praise the Lord.
And, people, I was blessed in the red, red blood
And I was raised upon the thorn.

II

The Butcher Son and Grandfather Bones

A weak soul does not have the endurance to resist the flesh for very long. It grows heavy, becomes flesh itself, and the contest ends.

—Nikos Kazantzakis, *The Last Temptation of Christ*

To our strongest drive, the tyrant in us, not only our reason bows but also our conscience.

—Friedrich Nietzsche, *Beyond Good and Evil*

Everything comes from everything, and everything is made out of everything, and everything returns into everything, because whatever exists in the elements is made out of those elements.

—Leonardo Da Vinci, *The Notebooks of Leonardo Da Vinci*

Grandfather Bone Say

Butcher Son hate to run but run
cause he afeard of voices in da world
of death by failure heart or otherwise
by cancer in da lung in da mind by
lightning bolt woodpecker gorbellied time
by hate by lust by love undone.

Thinking. Run him once by Christine's
where um her ghost haunt the happy
swimming pool. Herself self-drowned.
Once to Butcher Son she say in session ruminate
not thinking-fears over-abundant thought
water in da lungs.

Runs him now past the dead poet his friend
Galloway dead when thirty eight   his body
a busted dam and rushed all diseases in.
And now the plum tree close his home
emptied its fruit to the street and squish.
Who'd dare eat dat footed plum?

Good Friday, 1980

When Butcher Son grandmother's Grand-am roll
into the driveway, Butcher Son know noon now
and votive candles burn and rosaries lie beneath

Butcher Lady's eight by ten of Christ.
Butcher Son leave Superman in mid-flight
or Batman in mid-punch and all bad guys

equipoised in fear for three hours
until The Butcher—up to his wrists
in blood—came home and wash

and Christ give up the ghost Butcher Lady say
as she pinch each bead blue fingertip
crawl   eyes tight   through each decade

Our Savior and our Lord, she say at three
and say to Butcher Son *He died for your sins.*
Thank Him by not fidgeting. But Butcher Son

concerned for Superman who would be tricked
into kryptonite cage and for The Butcher new blood
and his thumb chunk black as rosary beads

Graceland

Mommy, I saw Elvis.
Did you?
Yes, but he's gone.

—John Strausbaugh

Butcher Lady walk past the backlit stained-glass
that glimmer in red, blue and green like a 70s
disco-tech and evoke a Holy Land night-life
hip-shaking sacrifice to pause before the bronzed
votive plaque that marks Elvis's grave.
A hush haunts the air.

The same hush that haunted
Dario Mendoza's nineteen-eighty-four Firebird
when the Virgin Mary guest-appeared;
the same goose-bump energy that baked
Jesus's crucifixion into a flour tortilla in New Mexico;
that spun his sunken face in a forkful of spaghetti
on a Texas billboard; that dropped into the soul
of Elvis impersonator Gregg Peters,

forcing diners at the Memphis Brauhaus to claim
that *something entered the room. Something
entered him, transforming him into something
taller, sexier.* And for a few shimmering moments
Peters (or should we call him the King now?) raised
the audience to its feet, screaming for his scarf
blessed with the sweat from his Presley-ian pores.

Butcher Lady shakes her head:
What kind of a mother is she anyway?
Dizzy with the pelvis-pumped
boogie-woogie of an Elvis impersonator
and crack-pot sightings of Mary and Jesus
when she should pray for her son
who chops wood in Montana and doesn't pray,
for her parish priest who decided his homosexuality
made him unfit for his collar, for the kingdom,

for The Butcher, for herself, for her faith,
because these dizzying flashes, this hush,
could make a woman what?
weep? hum *Love Me Tender?*
see a side-burned, lip-snarled face form in window

As God Was, America Was,
Say the Butcher Son,

a good idea. So was
the Third Reich, thought
they of the kingdom.
And Israel. Christianity.
Islam. Not to mention
Buddhism. —Shit, Boy, say Bones, many
we is think you bad, son.

Loosen yorself. Look down.
Cross yorself no mo?
What crown up yo
head weigh like dat of Solomon?
Thorns of woe
only one head God gave to carry.
—But think on the chair of Plato

(sunlight in the saddle of
the hill): doesn't matter now
—material or shadow—
what either final cause
each the other was.
—Butcher son, you scares me.
You scares me what you show.

Sunday Morning, Butcher Son Thinks on Salvation

Not in the church I pass on runs.
Not in the litany nor in the storied windows.
Not in the marble stations, nor stiff iconography.
More like a woman full and living.
—Problem Butcher Son is yo thoughts.
Dey should be handled like da ejaculate
of da sweaty Catholic boy—spewed
in da sock and thrown in da wash cause
I knows da indecent filth in yo head
I knows da women sickness bid you run,
will not let you eat, not sleep, not talk
But prevail and work on yo shape, ruin
yo own voice and words bewitched in trance.
Discard da lousy sickness Butcher Son.
Set on yo foot. Reject da offense.
Dispossess da madness and da obstruction.
Like a woman full and living. Fierce and pluck.
Open and charged, fired hot in resolution.
Enduring and universal tremble in my bed.
The vow and communion of heaven and hell
and the sulphurous delight to which I'm lead.

A Deeper Darkness, Say Butcher Son,

Wakes at dawn, or before,
some shapeless panic
like these crows
perched in coffee trees,
like these leaves
heavy between earth and sky,
like this ghost-fog
forming over the lake.
Everything reflects formless

and blurs lives into hydro-imagery.
Like Christ framed mid-ascension
between yesterday and today
and a future nobody exists in.
Like these leaves.
Like these crows.
Between something and nothing
to concretize the dead
and burn away the fog.

Grandfather Bone Say

Butcher Son think he prefer not to be,
say, dis red-tail hawk who's flying hard
against the harder winds, suspended,
without progress, forward nor backward.
An idea stuck in da mind.

He prefer not to be dis bird
whose will, though strong, smart,
is too fixed to rest in dat forgotten tree.
Branches bending with da wind.
Roots (for now) holding da dirt.

Yet he think he prefer not to be
dat forgotten tree. Dose buds
have failed spring's expectation.
From da air dose roots (for now)
feel moisture and acceptance.

Rather he think he prefer to be
dat snake curled beneath dat forgotten tree
and caught in da eye of dat fixed bird
to give up him skin spring by spring
and deny himself him self-identity.

III

Love Create Me Fool

A lady's voice . . . called me where I dwelled
In Limbo—a day so blessed and fairly featured
I prayed her to command me.

—Dante Alighieri, *The Inferno*

This is the female form,
A divine nimbus exhales from it from head to foot,
It attracts with fierce undeniable attraction,
I am drawn by its breath as if I were no more than a
helpless vapor, all falls aside but myself and it.

—Walt Whitman, *Leaves of Grass*

What next I bring shall please thee, be assured,
Thy likeness, thy fit help, thy other self,
Thy wish, exactly to thy heart's desire.

—John Milton, *Paradise Lost*

Butcher Son Thinks on Love and Wounds

-for Monica Cissell

This bar bears the air of a bad marriage.
Only the last-call drinkers slouched in stools
and waitresses counting tips and time

remain in the deep brown-yellow of beer
ads and smoke, an amber glow
that lends the bar the haze of Dante's eighth

where *horned demons with great whips*
beat naked *shades fiercely from behind.*
Butcher Son friend confesses, trepans, really,

a burr hole in his human skull to gush the sex
of sexpedition.com, all the women he's fucked,
that his wife's divorcing him, relieving

the dura mater of his pressurized marriage.
Butcher Son's own wife sleeps now, he knows,
deep in their marriage bed, one bare foot exposed,

and a pillow by her side because she says,
It makes me feel you there. And Butcher Son
would be as sweet if he wished him there.

The trepanned bone removed and charmed
and Butcher Son friend quotes Henry Miller
and George Battaille and other sensualists

to support his infidelity. The heart wants
what it wants but never fits its own wanting,
Butcher Son says, and assholes see the world

from behind dirty underwear, and our demon's
ass-cutting whips flake like ash, and Butcher Son
do wish himself beside her, all him seated inside her.

When My Son Asks Me

—adaptation of Bertolt Brecht's
Mein Junger Sohn Fragt Mich

When my son asks me
if he should study history
—what for, I want to tell him, to learn
Pax Americana will fall as other empires?

When my son asks me
if he should study mathematics
—why, I want to say, to learn
that one loaf of bread equals one loaf of bread?

When my son asks me
if he should study philosophy
—what for, I want to say,
Better to bury your head in the ground.

But when he asks me, yes, I'll say,
study history
study mathematics
study philosophy.

Us, Two

On the kitchen floor, the moonlight is spilled milk
is as line I wrote to confess what we two become

because what moves in us is not the pump and drive
sex-stirrings of legs-in-the-air muscle-tense passion

but the unpaid and unpayable bills,
the dying flowers and vegetables in the garden,

the whimpering hiccups of a two-year-old
who wept himself to sleep.

We deserve better than this.
We deserve to be stray spheres

finding each other's gravities and orbits,
lovers in darkness combusting milky ways.

But on the kitchen floor, the moonlight
is spilled milk is a line I wrote.

Where Light Goes?

-for Guthrie Cissell

To nap in your young son's bed as he reads
is calming as anything I know. To fall
asleep, his scent in the pillow under you,

is to admit you have never felt so tired,
so consumed by your own body. To lie
here is to feel small, to realize that all

your obstacles and all your slip-tumbles
you force yourself to call your life nothing.

To breathe him in is to feel that you
don't have to know how you should feel,
that a world still exists where children

are free to wake you and ask you
when the sun fondly nods, *Papa?*

The Butcher Son Cuts on Language

The truth is, distance is safe.
Light-years separate galaxies;
and gravity, according to one theory,
drives them unreachable distances apart,
preventing nuclear-force collisions;
evolution erected an impenetrable wall of time
between us and our oo-ooing cousins;
and God scattered the citizens of Babel
from that place all over the earth,
confusing *the speech of all the earth.*
And Butcher Son's words, like a repelling magnet,
pushed his wife weeping into her pillow,
and Butcher Son to the couch for a re-run
of *Star Trek: The Next Generation.*

Captain Jean Luc Picard and the Enterprise crew
face maximum shields to maximum shields, photon
torpedoes full, with an unintelligible
and possibly hostile species called the Tamarians.
After several failed communications—the universal
translator transposing terse Tamarian phrases
that mean nothing to Picard—the Tamarians
(obviously possessing superior technology)
beam Picard to a distant planet called Kalad-drell,
where Jean Luc, when his molecules pull back in,
finds the Tamarian captain prepared to engage
in what seems to Jean Luc captain to captain combat.
The Tamarian, armed with two knives, spreads his arms:
Darmok and Jallard at Tanagra and tosses Picard a knife.

Who refuses it, not wanting to risk war.
The Tamarian captian, confused and disappointed,
retrieves his weapon and withdraws from Picard,
declaring as he turns, *Shaka, when the walls fell.*
Night. Picard and the Tamarian burn separate fires.

Another theory: the universe can only expand so far
before its own gravity pulls it in on itself,
deflating it like a balloon
back to its original, immense mass and dust,
until, under its own weight, its central mass
burns white, and after some abortive attempts,
bursts into radiance, *a sustained thermonuclear fire*
that unfolds, like a rose, *the atoms and grains*
that make up galactic evolution.
A new beginning.
And no dispute dispels the fact
that chimps manipulate hundreds of signs
so that now the lixigram-literate Kanzi
fingers the command *Elizabeth apple cut,*
making our oo-ooing cousins not-so-distant.
And the citizens of Babel, confused as we are,
translate each other's poetry and scripture,
learning that our passions equal
the height of the original tower's and our depths
as low as Hell.

And my wife sleeps,
and it's morning on Kalad-drell.
A native beast of the planet,
another world's Grendel—ferocious, invisible—
attacks Picard and injures the Tamarian,

who offers Jean Luc the knife a second time,
saying, *Timba, his arms wide.*
Picard, an astute learner, begins to see,
and when he does, the Tamarian, relieved,
shouts *His eyes open.* But the alien
captain is dying, and Picard, to save
himself and the Federation, needs more,
Timba, his arms wide, he says.
The Tamarian captain, sputtering and weak,
recounts a Tamarian legend of companionship
and cooperation and friendship that builds worlds.
Darmok on the ocean. Tanagra on the ocean.
The beast at Tanagra. Jallard on the ocean.
Darmok and Jallard on the ocean.
Picard, now certain that the Tamarian's language
is built on metaphor understands. *His eyes open.*

It's morning now in Wichita,
a gray beast of a Monday morning,
and in the kitchen, the Butcher Son and his wife
stand maximum shields to maximum shields,
photon torpedoes armed and phasers on stun,
know the light years between them,
the expansive distances and unintelligible language,
but there's a pull they know, too.

Romeo in the garden. Juliet on the balcony.
Raskolnikov and Sonia in Siberia.
Butcher Son and Mim in the Kitchen.

IV

Prattling Poets

Poetry is an echo, asking a shadow to dance.

—Carl Sandburg

Some people go to priests; others to poetry;
I to my friends.

—Virginia Woolf

Immature poets imitate; mature poets steal.

—T. S. Eliot

My Friend Is a Fish

for Steve Johnson

There is nothing to hold, nothing
but the language of movement.
This is the whole of being totem.
To voice through the body
what the mind would speak.

Inside a Dying Letter to a Dead Friend

for Scott Galloway (1972-2012)

The poem I should have written
is the meat I should have eaten
before the letter from my therapist arrived,
before I read that she died.
Of course she committed suicide,
a death as cliché as rhyme.

So Scott,
I was too tired to eat.
The meat rotted
the stink inside my head.

The poem I should have written
is the funeral I attended
in Iowa under ice and snow
in the Episcopal church one hundred years old
made of stone.   My father-in-law
lay embalmed, a daintily painted doll
at our backs. Before us my niece born again.
The setting sun shone on her golden head.
A girlchild, a cherub, adorable
some said
an angel baptized at her grandfather's funeral.

So Scott,
I get it.
Alpha and Omega:
The old man's corpse inside the coffin.
The child's wet face inside the light.
In the old stone church, the old story told
of the golden orb that descends again
upon the winter solstice,
but rosy months will ascend
in spring time still before us.

The poem I should have written
is your wife and daughter left behind.
So, Scott, your ghost-mind
I know would grow your bones,
stuff your frame full of organs,
stitch your veins and sinews,
through your deep muscle,
re-stretch your skin,
and shake the dirt from your golden hair,
if you could,
to touch them.

So, here, Scott,
where we are,
where therapists swallow pills,
where old men die of cancer,
young men too,

where children are anointed
in the fading sun,
it's almost Christmas,
the festival of lights
the darkest time of year,
the flashy cliché,
the poems we have written.

The Dharma

—for Chet Gresham

Not from reverence
nor profound approbation
do you slip off
sandals and bend
before this plastic
stature of Siddhartha

But to clean
the filter in your pond
and to balance
on these slippery rocks.
This the footing and backbone.
This the universal truth.

Wallace Stevens, Elizabeth Bishop
My Friends and I at Land Between the Lakes

This isn't Stevens' ocean nor his idea of ocean;
this lake isn't Bishop's gas-colored bight.

Stevens refuses to step from my car,
and Bishop wets not a hand. *It'll burn,* she says.

So what are we to do with Lake Barkley,
those half-perceived coffee trees or oaks or kanji?

Barkley is stained with the orange flame
of campfires, the color of 7-Up and Maker's

Its water invites nets and lures, beckons
to speak Boudelaire and hear marimba in waves.

We'll hike its woods and bum these hills
and plunge into Barkey's burning water

without fear to sing no incantations of light,
no mumbo-jumbo for memory's thirst.

In my car, Bishop is drunk,
There are too many waterfalls here,

and Stevens stares into a deeper darkness
listening for his lady to sing.

Kootenai Peak, Montana

—for Steve Johnson

The wild up here is not forest wild;
it's not wild found in stone or moss.
Up here, the wild is not predator.
Up here my soul is unfathomable.
Sees itself in all time, healed.
Up here, nothing but world;
every lift of the head, every gaze,
every too-looked-for thing—world.

Lunch at Georgy Porgy's with Albert

—for Albert Goldbarth

Death'll kill you, and life'll kill you, and
all of us will opened one day
found lined with a tincture of Muenster.

        —Cheese by Albert Goldbarth

Georgy Porgy's'll kill you, the grease sink
of grease sinks: menus glutted
with various melted-animal-fat eatable:
fried venison haunch, heart-clogging cow,

and let's not forget those curdled, artery-choking
cheeses. The walls themselves tinctured
like the inside of a Goldbarthian belly:
egg-yolk yellow, amoeboid, sagging.

And Albert'll kill you. Your brain gooey
and droopy and clogged with come-back
Goldbarthian witticisms. You think and
think until gray matter oozes and tints

the inside of your skull with a grease
Georgy Porgy would be happy to line
its walls with, and finally you retort
and vomit the freshest, wittiest lines

this side of life. And Albert sits there,
black hair seasoned gray and curdled
like peppered cottage cheese,
musing a morsel of muenster.

V

Sometime Shadow

Men go fishing all of their lives without knowing that it is not fish they are after.

—Henry David Thoreau

Early in the morning, Jesus stood on the shore, but the disciples did not realize that it was Jesus.
He called out to them, "Friends, haven't you any fish?"
"No," they answered.

—John 21: 4-5

We are shaped by our thoughts; we become what we think. When the mind is pure, joy follows like a shadow that never leaves.

—Buddha

How to Scream a Fish

—for Rohan Cissell

Although I've never heard them, Michael Cissell says
fish scream. He's seen his father slit
and start to gut one while
it's still alive . . . it screams then,
bringing it closer.

—Albert Goldbarth, *Far: An Etymology*

Did I say scream? Well, yes, I suppose
to the fantastic horror of a nine-year-old's
hyperbolic imaginings,
for the noise I heard when the oxygen inside
the fish my father removed from the cooler
to clean
escaped as my father gently pushed
the fish's body, and gas pushed out
from the fish's gaping jaw and bulbous eyes
and bloody gills, *scream* is a good word.

And I'd want to say,
at that precise moment,
in Hollywood slow motion,
the fish's leaky bulbous eye caught my own.
I was hooked, we could say, pulled closer in.
And twelve mossy brown lines hung
like scrolls from the fish's fat blue lip.

Twelve epics of aquatic battles with the taut lines
of air breathers, narrow escapes
and harrowing fear and pain.
Victory and wisdom beneath each scar.
And there a thirteenth line that ends
with that scream and a boy yanked
from the fish's storyline,
like being pulled back through a nightmare
or a vortex of violent water,
to his father's voice:
Did you hear that?
Did you hear his spine crack?
That's when you tilt your blade, like this, and slide
it along the bone line slowly, smoothly
through the tail. And in one guiding swipe,
my father cleaned away the fish's entire body,
flipped the fish over and cut again.
He tossed the filets into a bowl of water
the head, spine and tail into a bucket.
That's how you clean a fish.

I'd want to write that,
and fill the poem with Paleolithic artifacts
found in southern Africa and the archeologist
who discovered the bones and rock scratchings
(clearly a human shape fishing
with a smaller human shape)

and Egyptian hieroglyphs depicting women
carrying reed baskets each with fish heads
sticking considerably out.
(I'd put twelve fish in those baskets, too,
for the sake of poetic union and trust my readers
to make the connection.)
I'd expect Jesus feeding the masses who crowded
the sea, Jesus *fishing for men*
(turns out he fished for twelve),
and the Jesus fish my students and their parents
proudly display on their pick-up truck bumpers.
From thirty thousand BCE
to contemporary ICT in a few lines.
And I'd pull that fish through every line
to finally place it clean on my readers' plates.
Salted to taste. And a reminder
that astrologists say we live now in the Age of Pisces,
Twelfth House of the Sun, the Fish House.

But this poem isn't made of fish, really,
nor the wisdom of metaphor,
nor plain religious poetic numbers
like twelve and thirteen,
or sudden fishy shamanistic closeness to primitive life
and epiphany of universal atom-based *togetherness*
in which we're all just ONE fish. Much simpler:
a father cast a life line, tossed out an old attempt
at *close* and *together,* by teaching his son to fish;
and the son who never fished with his father again.

Not once after, that I remember. We could say,
I didn't take the bait. We could say
my father cast in shallow waters. Lost his patience.
Switched lures. Cast once more and quit the spot.
We could also say that I

tried to read Goldbarth's lines to my nine-year-old son.
To show my name caught in those lines.
To reel my son in, we could say.
To share a world of language from which I draw
so much peace and pleasure and unity and. . . .
He broke my line with a simple shrug.
One motion. And he was off my hook.
The linguistic possibilities!
The exaggerated symbolism!
The vacuous silence of the gaping fish mouth!
The all-knowing eye of the fish!
The vortex of violent water as you're pulled
into the terrible reality of oxygen!
Did you hear my spine crack?
Did you hear me scream?

Michael Cissell lives in Wichita, KS.

This project was made possible, in part, by generous support from the Osage Arts Community.

Osage Arts Community provides temporary time, space and support for the creation of new artistic works in a retreat format, serving creative people of all kinds — visual artists, composers, poets, fiction and nonfiction writers. Located on a 152-acre farm in an isolated rural mountainside setting in Central Missouri and bordered by ¾ of a mile of the Gasconade River, OAC provides residencies to those working alone, as well as welcoming collaborative teams, offering living space and workspace in a country environment to emerging and mid-career artists. For more information, visit us at www.osageac.org

Osage Arts Community